HAL•LEONARD®
PIANO PLAY-ALONG

AUDIO ACCESS INCLUDED

PIANO | VOCAL | GUITAR ▪ AUDIO   **VOLUME 130**

WEST SIDE STORY

Music by **Leonard Bernstein®**   Lyrics by **Stephen Sondheim**

CONTENTS

T0078891

To access audio visit:
www.halleonard.com/mylibrary

Enter Code
2278-0915-1416-8642

ISBN 978-1-4803-9674-6

LEONARD BERNSTEIN
Music Publishing
Company LLC

BOOSEY & HAWKES

IMAGEM MUSIC

DISTRIBUTED BY
HAL•LEONARD®

Visit Hal Leonard Online at
www.halleonard.com

AMERICA

Lyrics by STEPHEN SONDHEIM
Music by LEONARD BERNSTEIN

Moderately bright

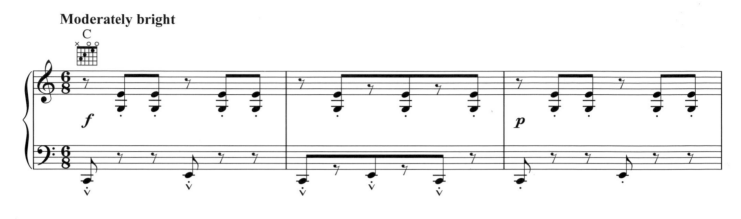

Lightly

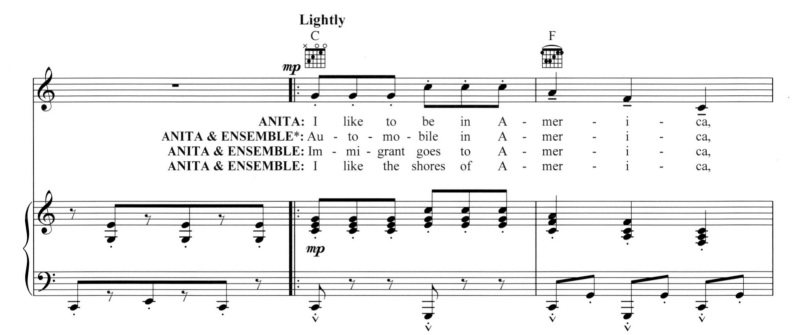

ANITA: I like to be in A - mer - i - ca,
ANITA & ENSEMBLE*: Au - to - mo - bile in A - mer - i - ca,
ANITA & ENSEMBLE: Im - mi - grant goes to A - mer - i - ca,
ANITA & ENSEMBLE: I like the shores of A - mer - i - ca,

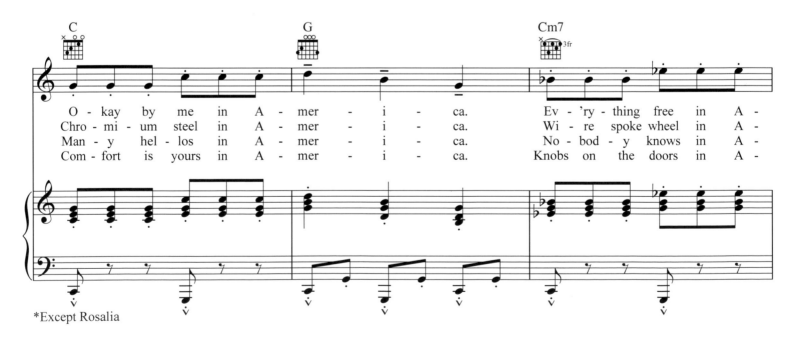

O - kay by me in A - mer - i - ca. Ev - 'ry - thing free in A -
Chro - mi - um steel in A - mer - i - ca. Wi - re spoke wheel in A -
Man - y hel - los in A - mer - i - ca. No - bod - y knows in A -
Com - fort is yours in A - mer - i - ca. Knobs on the doors in A -

*Except Rosalia

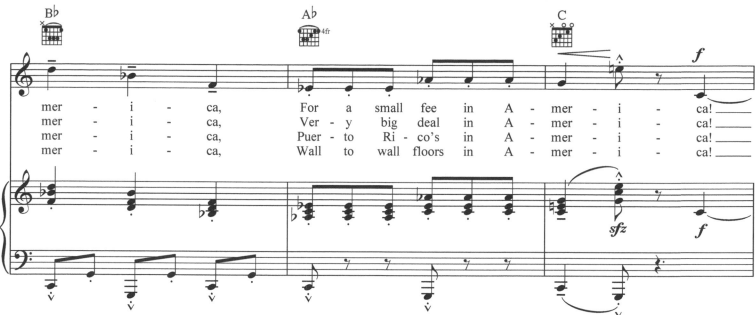

mer - i - ca, For a small fee in A - mer - i - ca! _____
mer - i - ca, Ver - y big deal in A - mer - i - ca! _____
mer - i - ca, Puer - to Ri - co's in A - mer - i - ca! _____
mer - i - ca, Wall to wall floors in A - mer - i - ca! _____

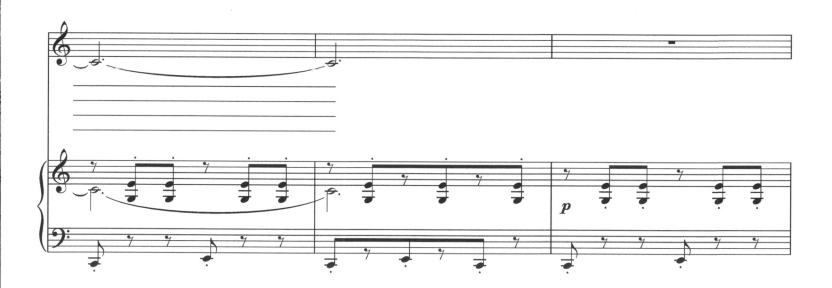

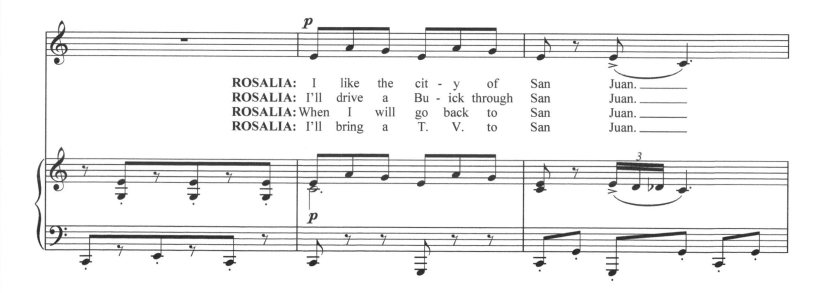

ROSALIA: I like the cit - y of San Juan. _____
ROSALIA: I'll drive a Bu - ick through San Juan. _____
ROSALIA: When I will go back to San Juan. _____
ROSALIA: I'll bring a T. V. to San Juan. _____

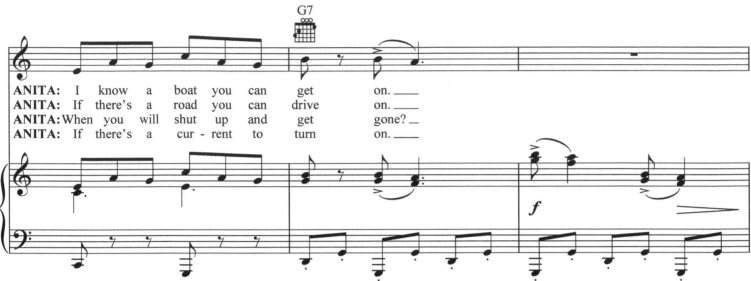

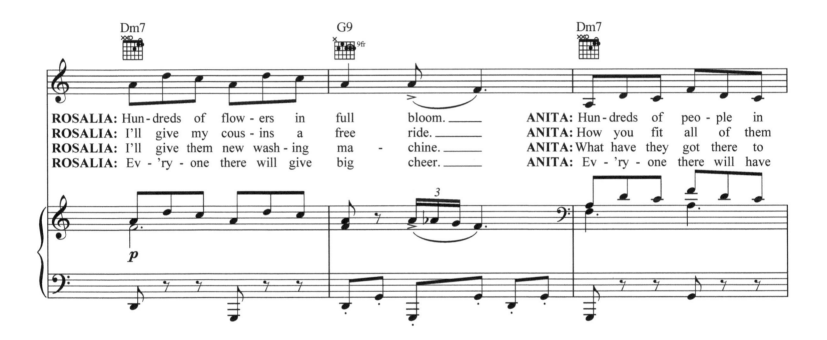

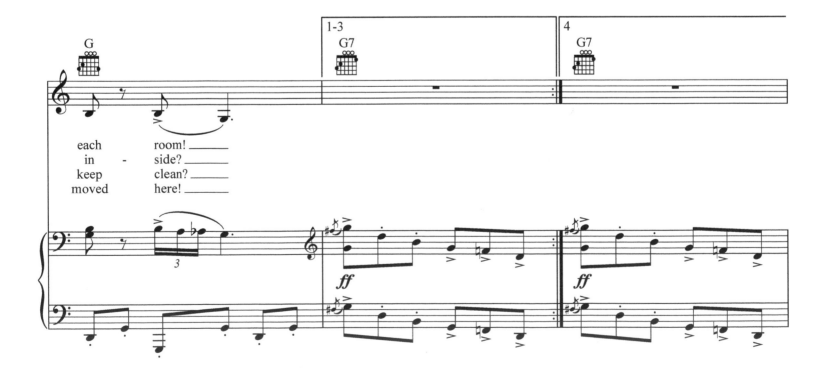

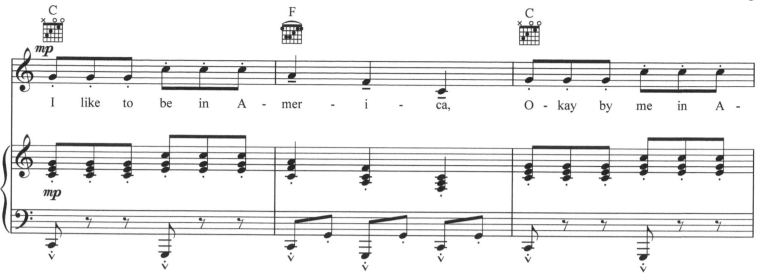

I like to be in A - mer - i - ca, O - kay by me in A -

mer - i - ca. Ev - 'ry - thing free in A - mer - i - ca,

For a small fee in A - mer - i - ca! _____

COOL

Lyrics by STEPHEN SONDHEIM
Music by LEONARD BERNSTEIN

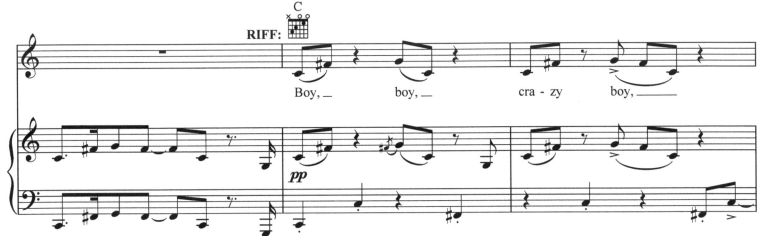

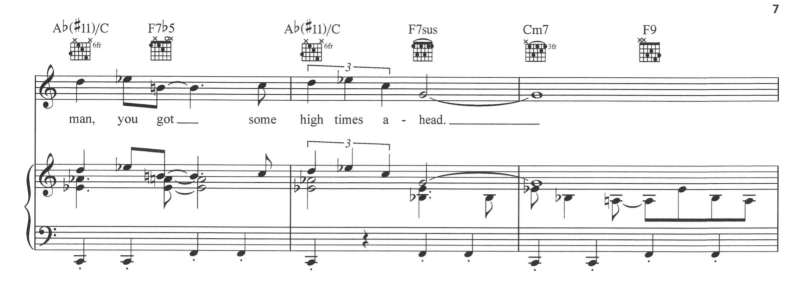

man, you got ___ some high times a - head. _____

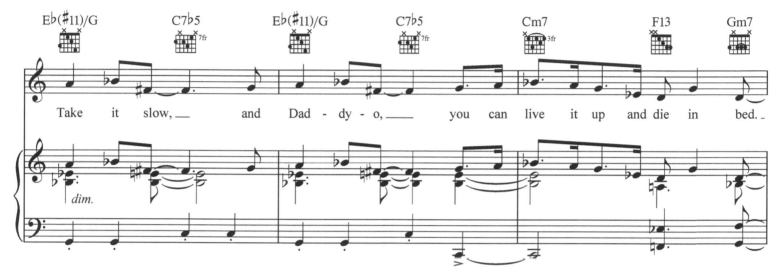

Take it slow, __ and Dad - dy - o, ___ you can live it up and die in bed. _

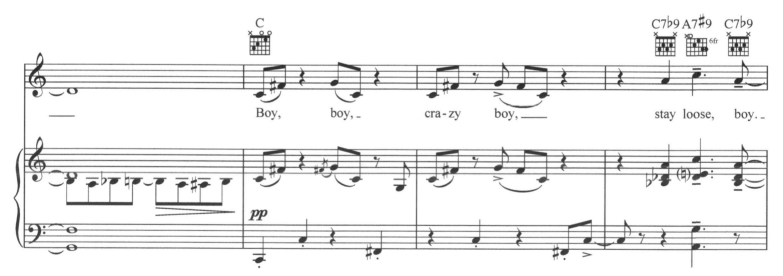

__ Boy, boy, _ cra - zy boy, ___ stay loose, boy. _

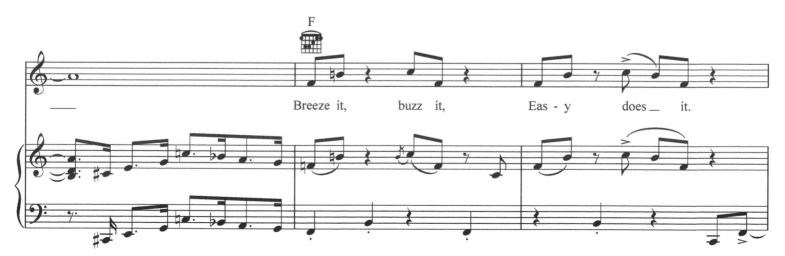

Breeze it, buzz it, Eas - y does _ it.

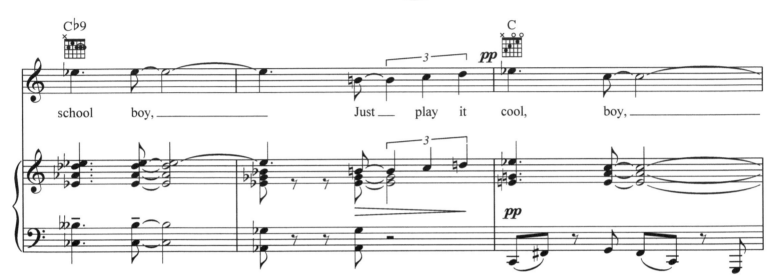

Turn off the juice, _____ boy. Go, man, go, ___ but not like a yo - yo

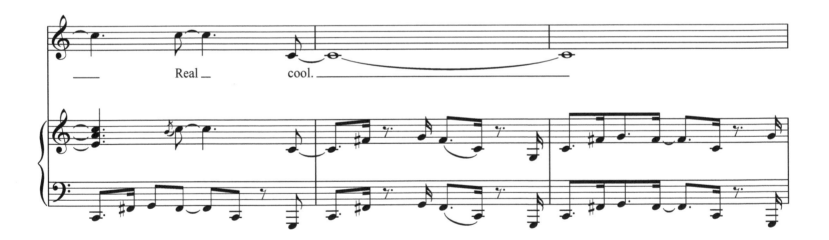

school boy, _____ Just ___ play it cool, boy, _____

Real __ cool. _____

MARIA

Lyrics by STEPHEN SONDHEIM
Music by LEONARD BERNSTEIN

Slowly and freely

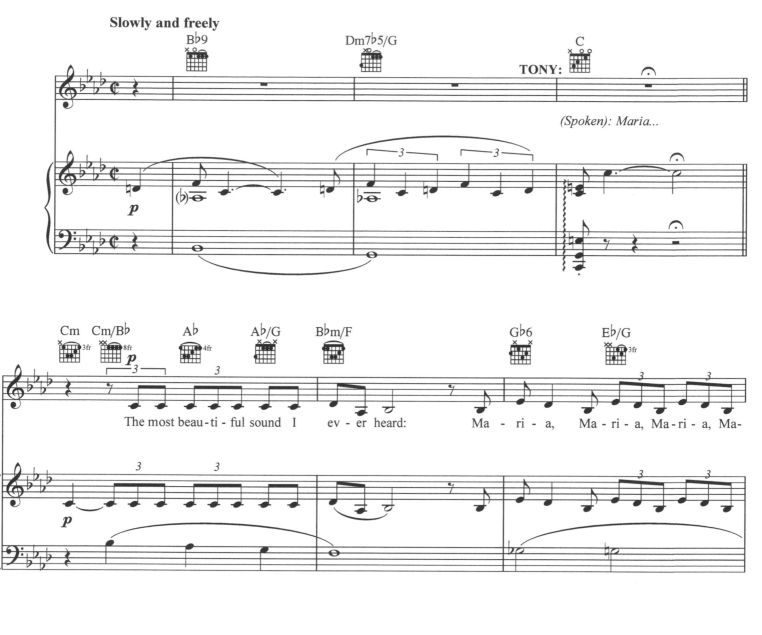

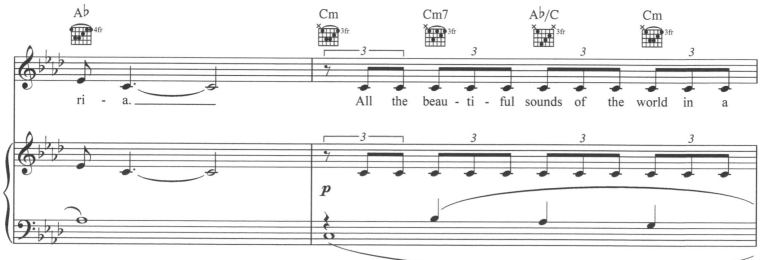

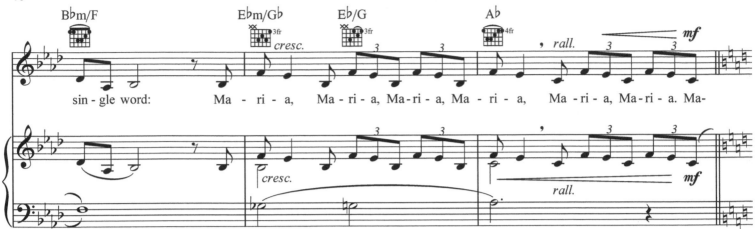

sin-gle word: Ma-ri-a, Ma-ri-a, Ma-ri-a, Ma-ri-a, Ma-ri-a, Ma-ri-a. Ma-

Moderately (warmly)

ri-a,_____ I've just met a girl named Ma-ri-a,_____ And

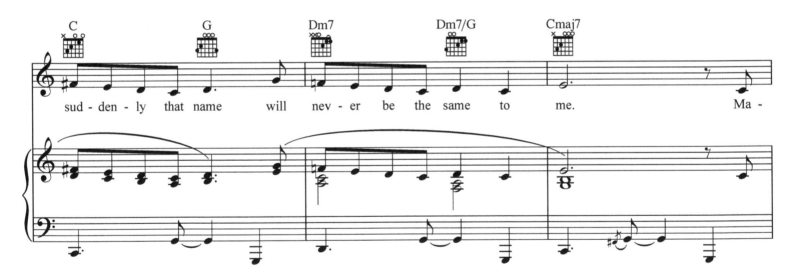

sud-den-ly that name will nev-er be the same to me. Ma-

ri-a,_____ I've just kissed a girl named Ma-ri-a,_____ And

* The extended version is used on the accompaniment track.

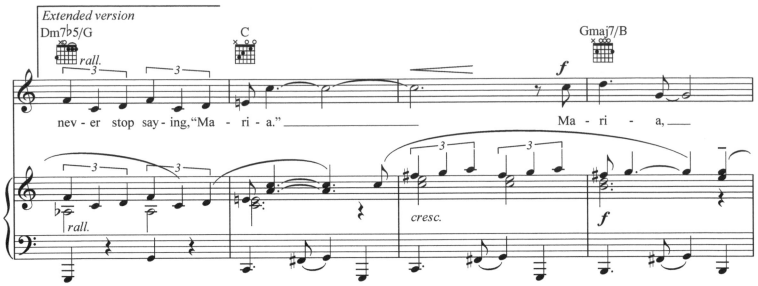

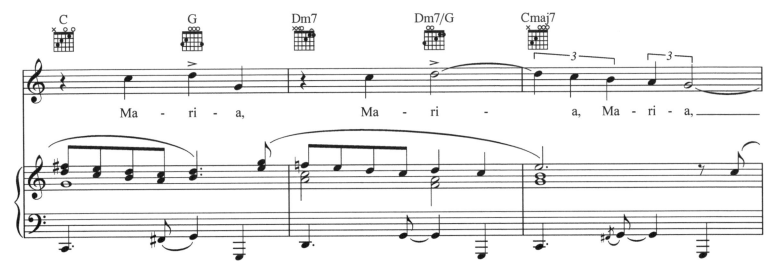

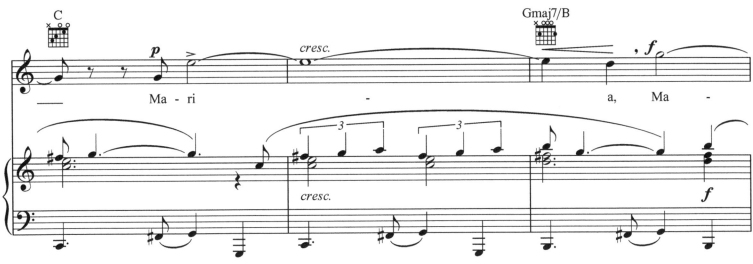

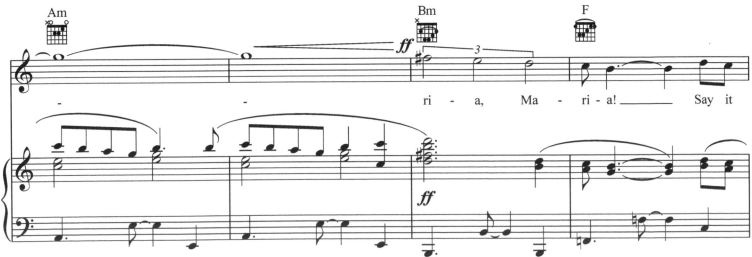

I FEEL PRETTY

Lyrics by STEPHEN SONDHEIM
Music by LEONARD BERNSTEIN

Originally an ensemble number, adapted here as a solo.

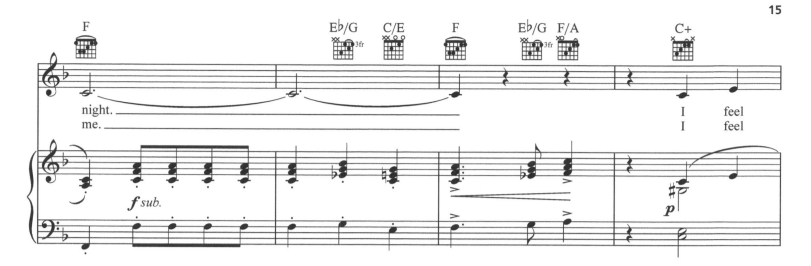

night. _____ I feel
me. _____ I feel

charm - ing, __ oh, so charm - ing, __ It's a - larm - ing how
diz - zy, __ I feel sun - ny, __ I feel fiz - zy and

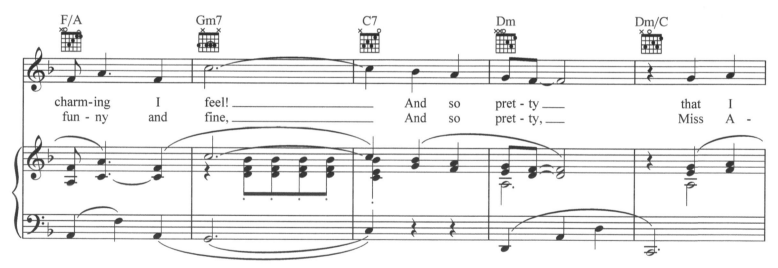

charm - ing I feel! _____ And so pret - ty __ that I
fun - ny and fine, _____ And so pret - ty, __ Miss A -

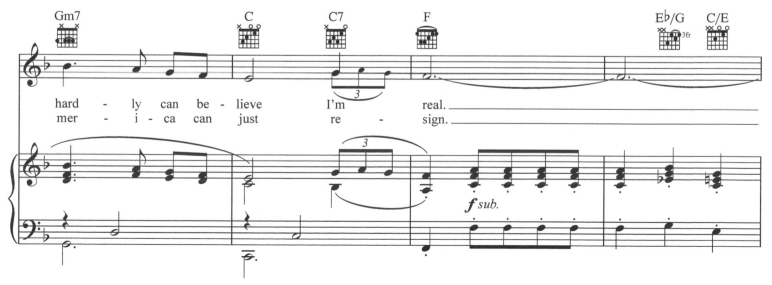

hard - ly can be - lieve I'm real. _____
mer - i - ca can just re - sign. _____

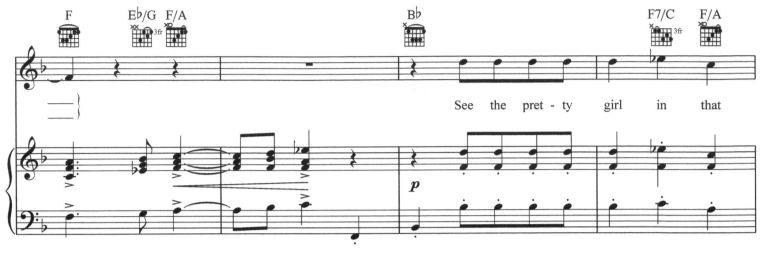

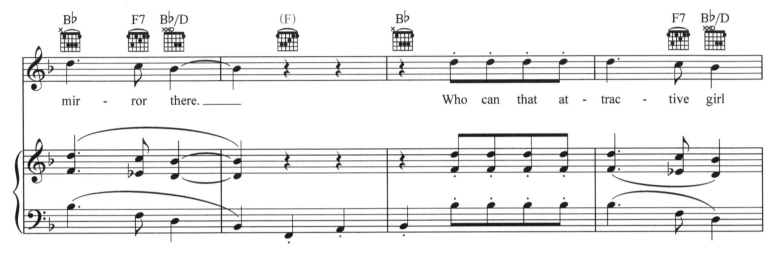

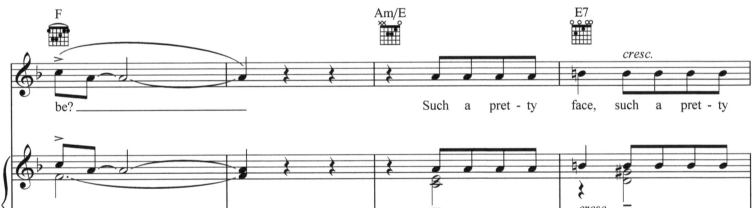

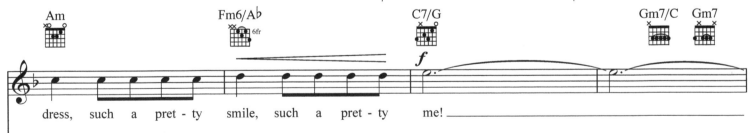

I feel stun-ning, _ and en-tranc-ing, _

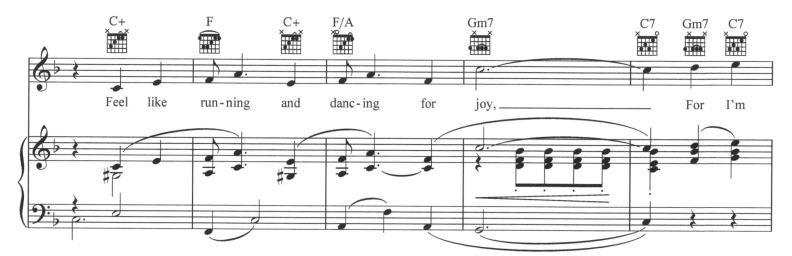

Feel like run-ning and danc-ing for joy, _____ For I'm

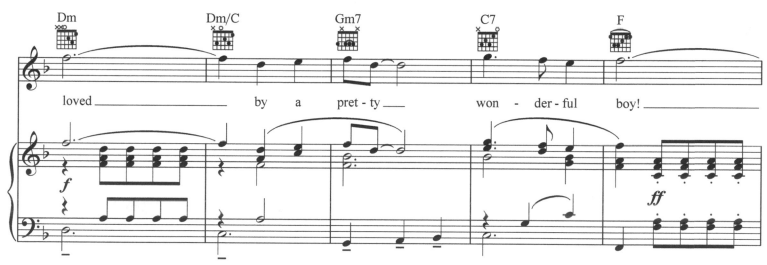

loved _____ by a pret-ty _ won-der-ful boy! _____

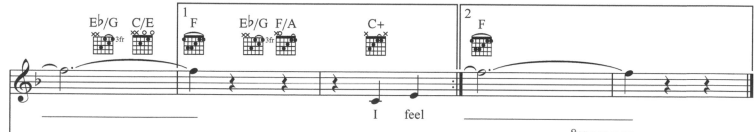

I feel

ONE HAND, ONE HEART

Lyrics by STEPHEN SONDHEIM
Music by LEONARD BERNSTEIN

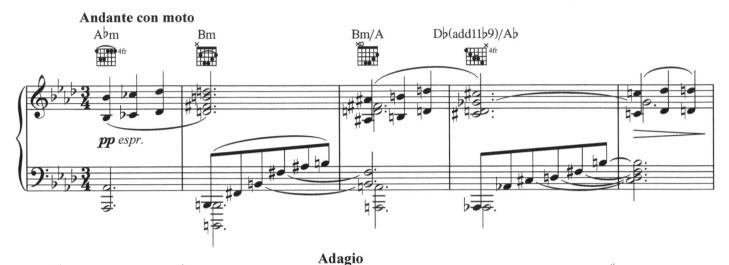

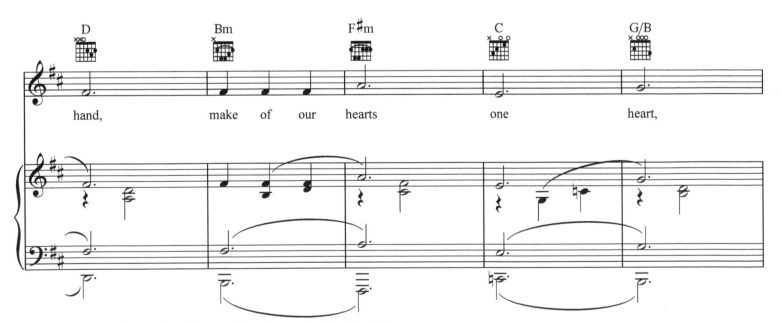

Originally a duet for Maria and Tony, adapted as a solo for this edition.

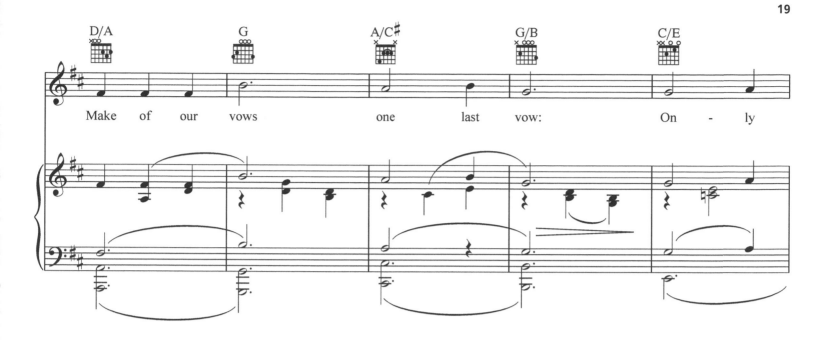

Make of our vows one last vow: On - ly

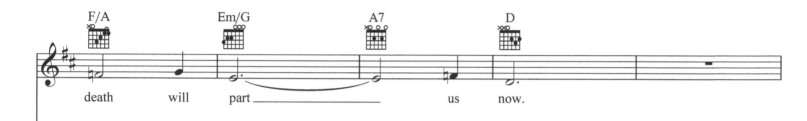

death will part _____ us now.

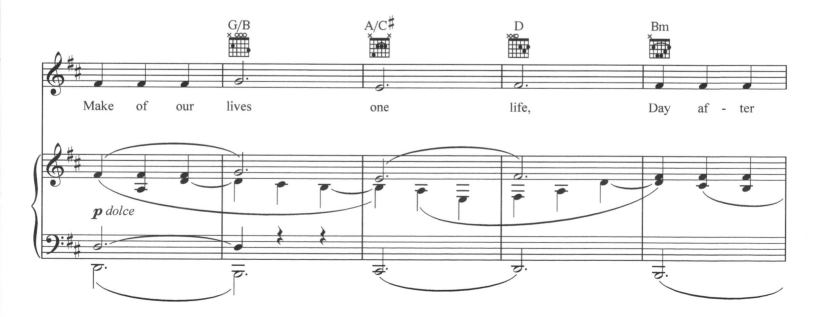

Make of our lives one life, Day af - ter

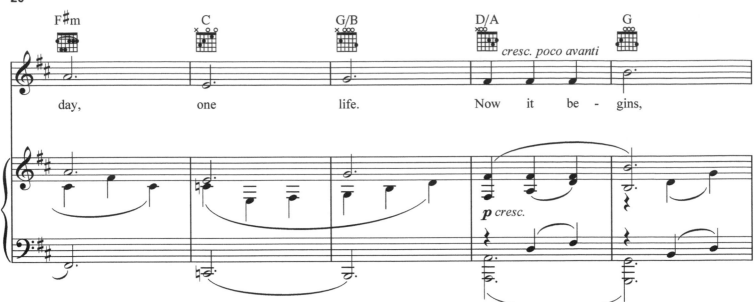

day,   one   life.   Now   it be - gins,

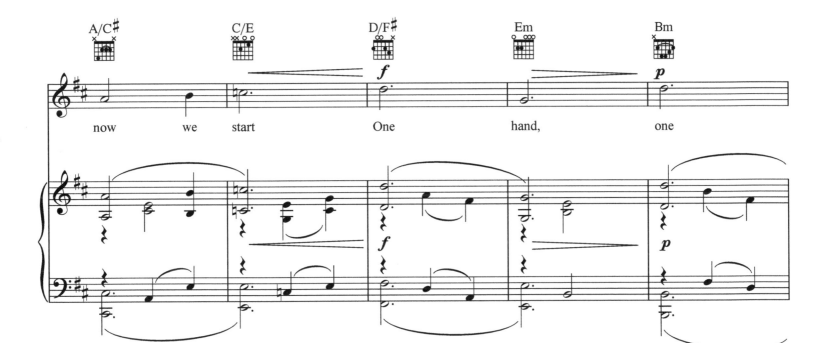

now   we   start   One   hand,   one

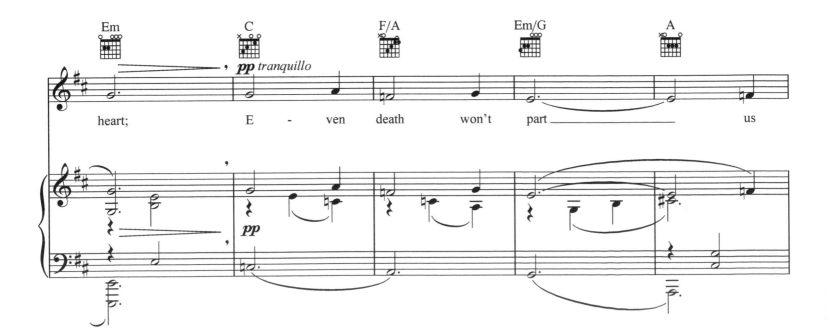

heart;   E - ven   death   won't   part _____   us

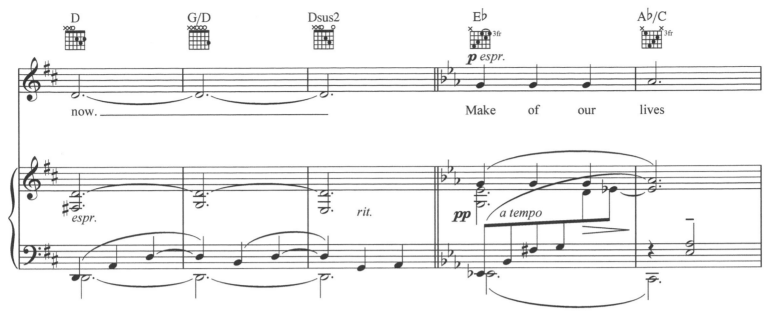

now. _____ Make of our lives

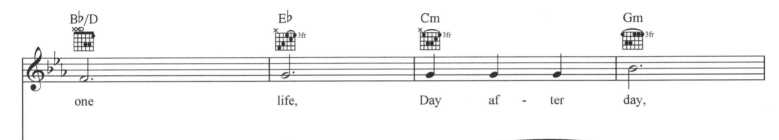

one life, Day af - ter day,

one life. Now it be - gins,

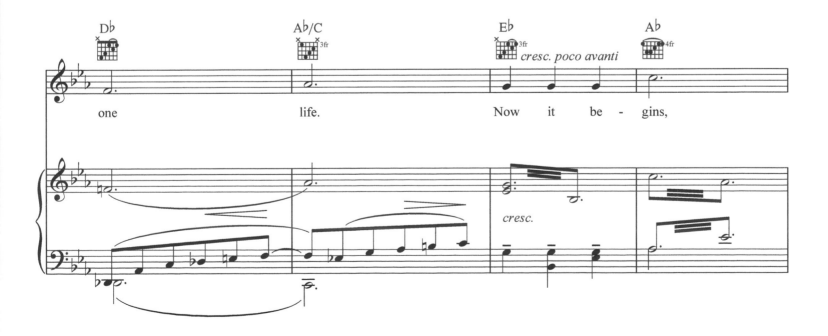

SOMETHING'S COMING

Lyrics by STEPHEN SONDHEIM
Music by LEONARD BERNSTEIN

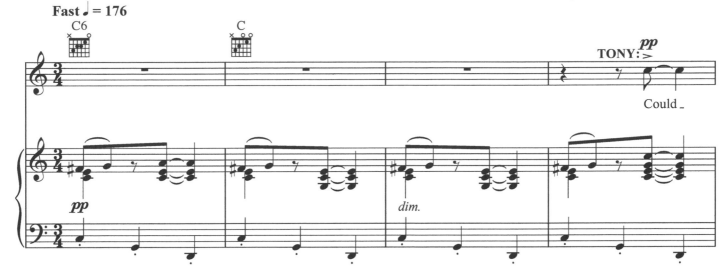

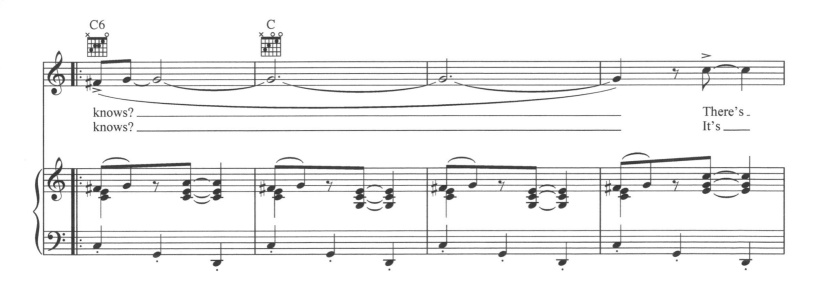

24

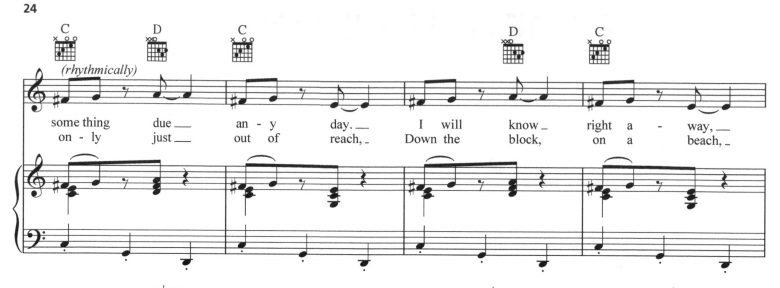

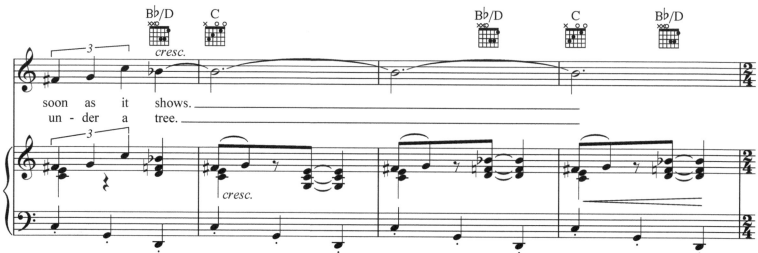

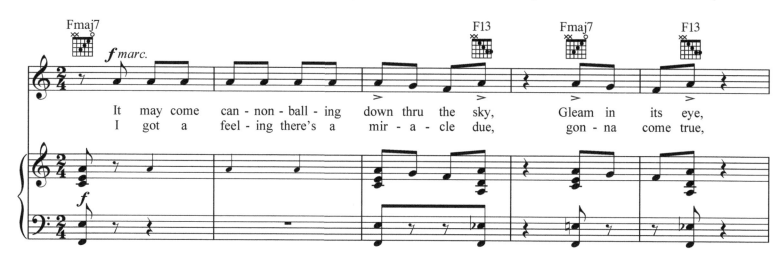

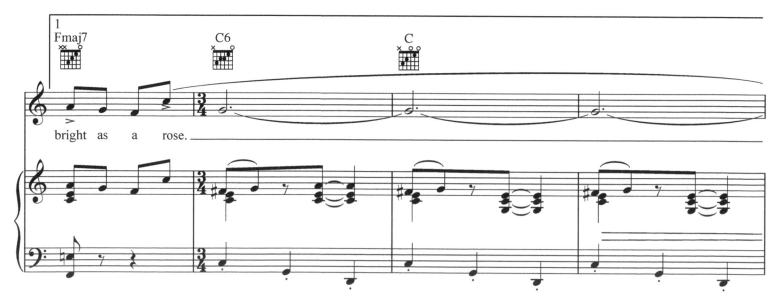

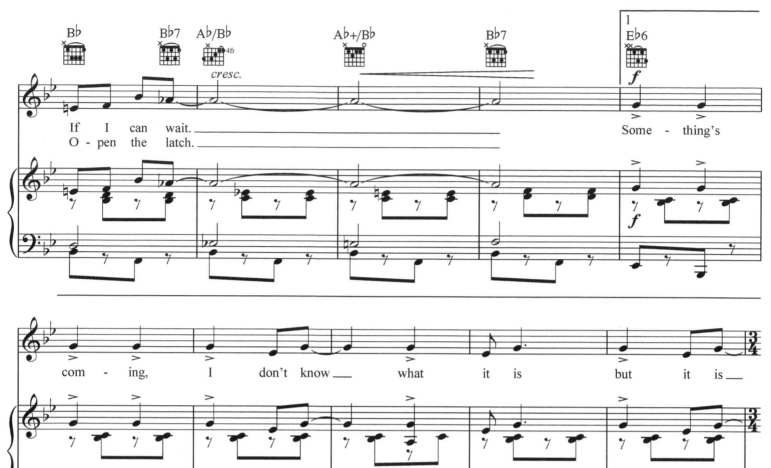

If I can wait. _____ Some - thing's
O - pen the latch. _____

com - ing, I don't know ___ what it is but it is ___

____ gon - na be great. _____

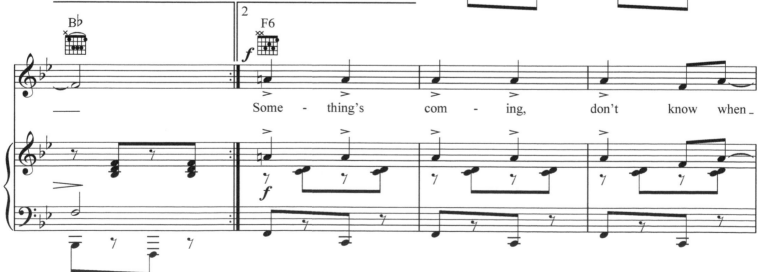

Some - thing's com - ing, don't know when ___

but it's soon; catch the moon,____ one-hand-ed catch.__

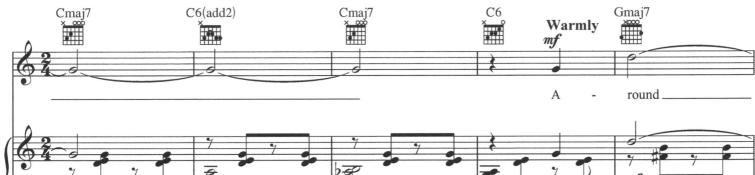

A - round____

the____ cor - ner,____

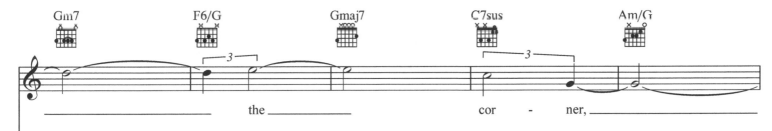

or whis - tling____ down____

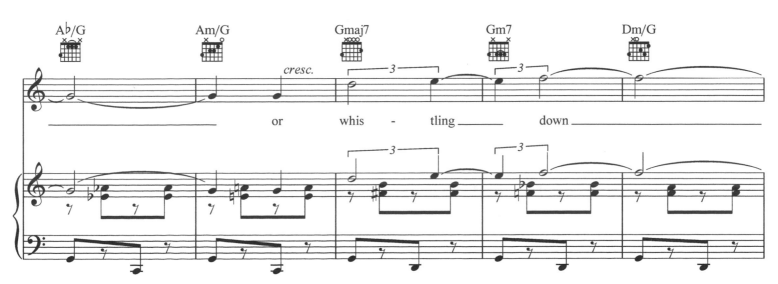

the riv - er. Come

on, de - liv - er

to me.

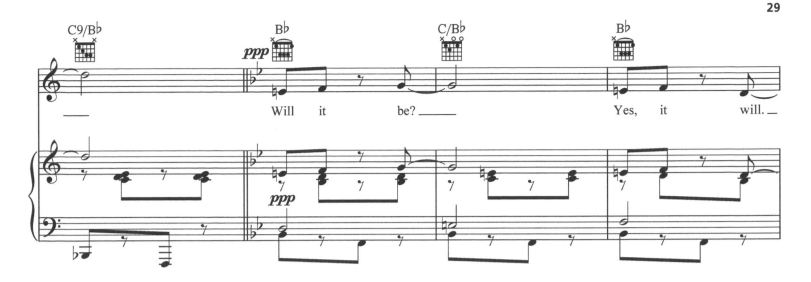

Will it be? _____ Yes, it will. _

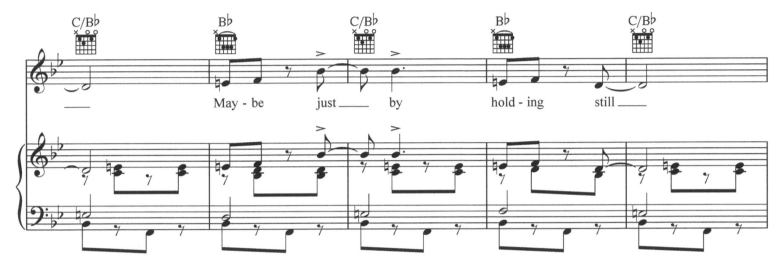

_____ May - be just _____ by hold - ing still _____

It - 'll be there. _____ Come on,

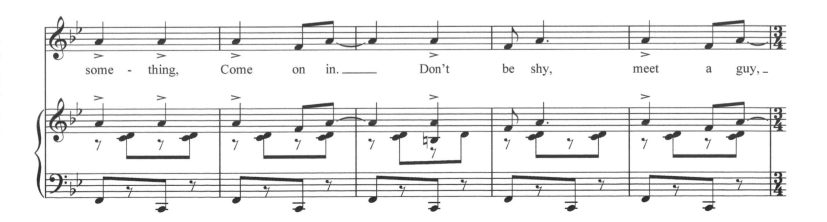

some - thing, Come on in. _____ Don't be shy, meet a guy, _

Pull up a chair. _____

The air _____ is _____

hum - ming, _____ And some - thing ___

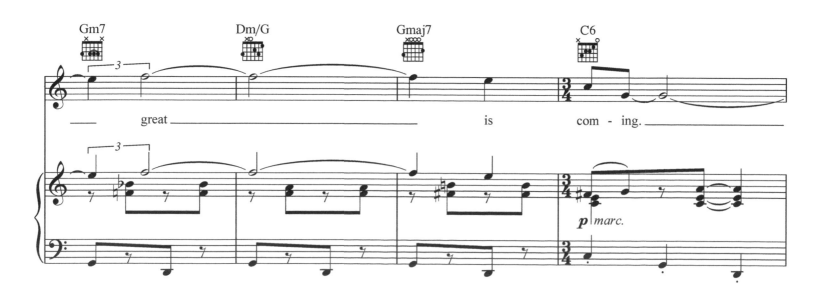

___ great _____ is com - ing. ___

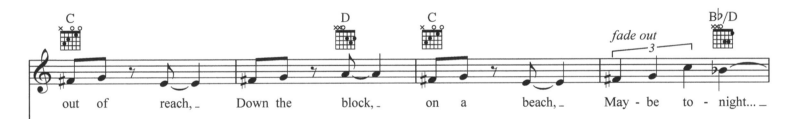

TONIGHT

Lyrics by STEPHEN SONDHEIM
Music by LEONARD BERNSTEIN

The complete number, "Balcony Scene," is a duet for Maria and Tony, adapted here as a solo.

night, to - night, I'll see my love to -

night. And for us stars will stop where they

are! _____ To - day the

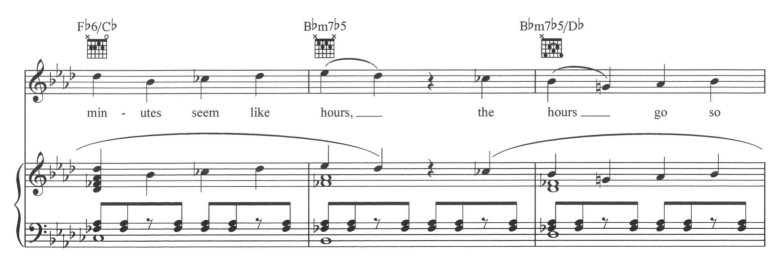

min - utes seem like hours, ____ the hours ____ go so

SOMEWHERE

Lyrics by STEPHEN SONDHEIM
Music by LEONARD BERNSTEIN

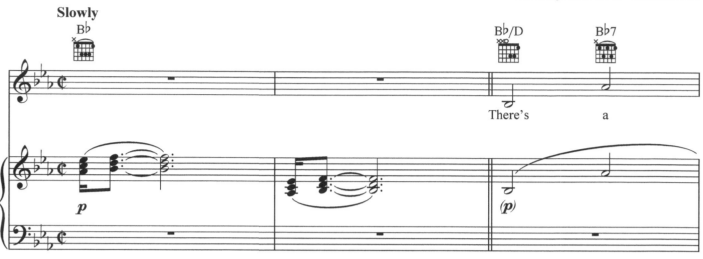

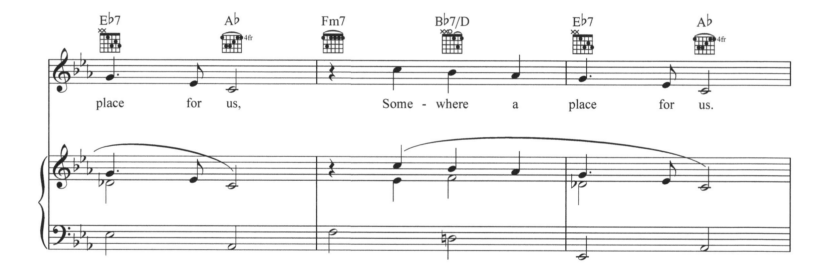

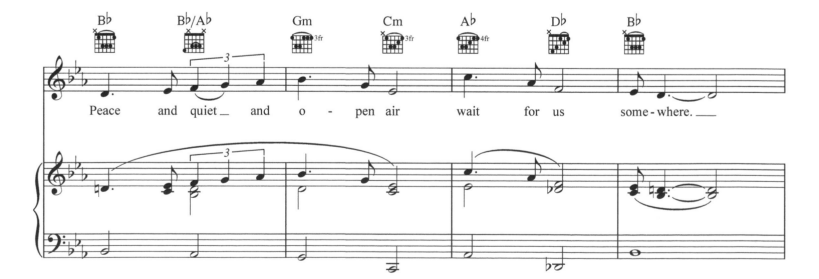

THE ULTIMATE SONGBOOKS

HAL•LEONARD®

PIANO PLAY-ALONG

These great songbook/audio packs come with our standard arrangements for piano and voice with guitar chord frames plus audio. The audio includes a full performance of each song, as well as a second track without the piano part so you can play "lead" with the band!

  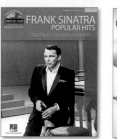    

BOOK/CD PACKS

1. **Movie Music** 00311072 .... $14.95
7. **Love Songs** 00311078 .... $14.95
12. **Christmas Favorites** 00311137 .... $15.95
15. **Favorite Standards** 00311146 .... $14.95
27. **Andrew Lloyd Webber Greats** 00311179 .... $14.95
28. **Lennon & McCartney** 00311180 .... $14.95
44. **Frank Sinatra – Popular Hits** 00311277 .... $14.95
71. **George Gershwin** 00102687 .... $24.99
77. **Elton John Favorites** 00311884 .... $14.99
78. **Eric Clapton** 00311885 .... $14.99
81. **Josh Groban** 00311901 .... $14.99
82. **Lionel Richie** 00311902 .... $14.99
86. **Barry Manilow** 00311935 .... $14.99
87. **Patsy Cline** 00311936 .... $14.99
90. **Irish Favorites** 00311969 .... $14.99
92. **Disney Favorites** 00311973 .... $14.99
97. **Great Classical Themes** 00312020 .... $14.99
98. **Christmas Cheer** 00312021 .... $14.99
105. **Bee Gees** 00312055 .... $14.99
106. **Carole King** 00312056 .... $14.99
107. **Bob Dylan** 00312057 .... $16.99
108. **Simon & Garfunkel** 00312058 .... $16.99
114. **Motown** 00312176 .... $14.99
115. **John Denver** 00312249 .... $14.99
123. **Chris Tomlin** 00312563 .... $14.99
125. **Katy Perry** 00109373 .... $14.99

BOOKS/ONLINE AUDIO

5. **Disney** 00311076 .... $14.99
8. **The Piano Guys – Uncharted** 00202549 .... $24.99
9. **The Piano Guys – Christmas Together** 00259567 .... $24.99
16. **Coldplay** 00316506 .... $17.99
20. **La La Land** 00241591 .... $19.99
24. **Les Misérables** 00311169 .... $14.99
25. **The Sound of Music** 00311175 .... $15.99
30. **Elton John Hits** 00311182 .... $16.99
31. **Carpenters** 00311183 .... $17.99
32. **Adele** 00156222 .... $24.99
33. **Peanuts™** 00311227 .... $17.99
34. **A Charlie Brown Christmas** 00311228 .... $16.99
46. **Wicked** 00311317 .... $17.99
62. **Billy Joel Hits** 00311465 .... $14.99
65. **Casting Crowns** 00311494 .... $14.99
69. **Pirates of the Caribbean** 00311807 .... $17.99
72. **Van Morrison** 00103053 .... $16.99
73. **Mamma Mia! – The Movie** 00311831 .... $17.99
76. **Pride & Prejudice** 00311862 .... $15.99
83. **Phantom of the Opera** 00311903 .... $16.99
113. **Queen** 00312164 .... $16.99
117. **Alicia Keys** 00312306 .... $17.99
126. **Bruno Mars** 00123121 .... $19.99
127. **Star Wars** 00110282 .... $16.99
128 **Frozen** 00126480 .... $16.99
130. **West Side Story** 00130738 .... $14.99
131. **The Piano Guys – Wonders** 00141503 (Contains backing tracks only) $24.99

HAL•LEONARD®

7777 W. BLUEMOUND RD. P.O. BOX 13819 MILWAUKEE, WI 53213

Order online from your favorite music retailer at
halleonard.com

Prices, contents and availability subject to change without notice

0322
276

THE NEW DECADE SERIES

Books with Online Audio • Arranged for Piano, Voice, and Guitar

The New Decade Series features collections of iconic songs from each decade with great backing tracks so you can play them and sound like a pro. You access the tracks online for streaming or download. **See complete song listings online at www.halleonard.com**

SONGS OF THE 1920s
Ain't Misbehavin' • Baby Face • California, Here I Come • Fascinating Rhythm • I Wanna Be Loved by You • It Had to Be You • Mack the Knife • Ol' Man River • Puttin' on the Ritz • Rhapsody in Blue • Someone to Watch over Me • Tea for Two • Who's Sorry Now • and more.
00137576 P/V/G....................................$27.99

SONGS OF THE 1930s
As Time Goes By • Blue Moon • Cheek to Cheek • Embraceable You • A Fine Romance • Georgia on My Mind • I Only Have Eyes for You • The Lady Is a Tramp • On the Sunny Side of the Street • Over the Rainbow • Pennies from Heaven • Stormy Weather (Keeps Rainin' All the Time) • The Way You Look Tonight • and more.
00137579 P/V/G....................................$24.99

SONGS OF THE 1940s
At Last • Boogie Woogie Bugle Boy • Don't Get Around Much Anymore • God Bless' the Child • How High the Moon • It Could Happen to You • La Vie En Rose (Take Me to Your Heart Again) • Route 66 • Sentimental Journey • The Trolley Song • You'd Be So Nice to Come Home To • Zip-A-Dee-Doo-Dah • and more.
00137582 P/V/G....................................$29.99

SONGS OF THE 1950s
Ain't That a Shame • Be-Bop-A-Lula • Chantilly Lace • Earth Angel • Fever • Great Balls of Fire • Love Me Tender • Mona Lisa • Peggy Sue • Que Sera, Sera (Whatever Will Be, Will Be) • Rock Around the Clock • Sixteen Tons • A Teenager in Love • That'll Be the Day • Unchained Melody • Volare • You Send Me • Your Cheatin' Heart • and more.
00137595 P/V/G....................................$29.99

SONGS OF THE 1960s
All You Need Is Love • Beyond the Sea • Born to Be Wild • California Girls • Dancing in the Street • Happy Together • King of the Road • Leaving on a Jet Plane • Louie, Louie • My Generation • Oh, Pretty Woman • Sunshine of Your Love • Under the Boardwalk • You Really Got Me • and more.
00137596 P/V/G $27.99

SONGS OF THE 1970s
ABC • Bridge over Troubled Water • Cat's in the Cradle • Dancing Queen • Free Bird • Goodbye Yellow Brick Road • Hotel California • I Will Survive • Joy to the World • Killing Me Softly with His Song • Layla • Let It Be • Piano Man • The Rainbow Connection • Stairway to Heaven • The Way We Were • Your Song • and more.
00137599 P/V/G $34.99

SONGS OF THE 1980s
Addicted to Love • Beat It • Careless Whisper • Come on Eileen • Don't Stop Believin' • Every Rose Has Its Thorn • Footloose • I Just Called to Say I Love You • Jessie's Girl • Livin' on a Prayer • Saving All My Love for You • Take on Me • Up Where We Belong • The Wind Beneath My Wings • and more.
00137600 P/V/G $34.99

SONGS OF THE 1990s
Angel • Black Velvet • Can You Feel the Love Tonight • (Everything I Do) I Do It for You • Friends in Low Places • Hero • I Will Always Love You • More Than Words • My Heart Will Go On (Love Theme from 'Titanic') • Smells like Teen Spirit • Under the Bridge • Vision of Love • Wonderwall • and more.
00137601 P/V/G $34.99

SONGS OF THE 2000s
Bad Day • Beautiful • Before He Cheats • Chasing Cars • Chasing Pavements • Drops of Jupiter (Tell Me) • Fireflies • Hey There Delilah • How to Save a Life • I Gotta Feeling • I'm Yours • Just Dance • Love Story • 100 Years • Rehab • Unwritten • You Raise Me Up • and more.
00137608 P/V/G $34.99

SONGS OF THE 2010s - Updated Edition
All About That Bass • Best Day of My Life • Cups (When I'm Gone) • Firework • Get Lucky • Happy • I Knew You Were Trouble • Just Give Me a Reason • Little Talks • The Middle • Perfect • Rolling in the Deep • Shallow • Stay with Me • There's Nothing Holdin' Me Back • Uptown Funk • Wake Me Up • and more.
00338996 P/V/G $29.99

halleonard.com